NINE FATHOM DEEP

David Constantine was born in 1944 in Salford, Lancashire. He read Modern Languages at Wadham College, Oxford, and lectured in German at Durham from 1969 to 1981 and at Oxford from 1981 to 2000. He is a freelance writer and translator, a Fellow of the Queen's College, Oxford, and co-editor with Helen Constantine of *Modern Poetry in Translation*. He lives in Oxford and Scilly.

Since his first collection *A Brightness to Cast Shadows* in 1980, all his poetry collections have been published by Bloodaxe Books. *Watching for Dolphins* (1983) won the Alice Hunt Bartlett Prize. *Madder* (1987), a Poetry Book Society Recommendation, won the Southern Arts Literature Prize; the French edition, translated by Yves Bichet as *Sorlingues* (Éditions La Dogana, 1992), won the Prix Rhône-Alpes du Livre. His *Selected Poems* (1991) was a Poetry Book Society Recommendation. *Caspar Hauser: a poem in nine cantos* (1994) was followed by *The Pelt of Wasps* (1998) and by *Something for the Ghosts* (Bloodaxe Books, 2002), which was shortlisted for the Whitbread Poetry Award. His most recent poetry titles are *Collected Poems* (2004), a Poetry Book Society Recommendation, and *Nine Fathom Deep* (2009).

He has published translations of poetry and prose by German, French and Greek writers. He was joint winner of the European Translation Prize in 1998 for his translation of Friedrich Hölderlin's *Selected Poems* (Bloodaxe Books, 1990; new edition, 1996), published a critical introduction to the poetry of Hölderlin (OUP, 1988), and translated Hölderlin's versions of Sophocles' *Oedipus* and *Antigone* as *Hölderlin's Sophocles* (Bloodaxe Books, 2001). His translation of Hans Magnus Enzensberger's *Lighter Than Air* (Bloodaxe Books, 2002) won the Poetry Society's Corneliu M Popescu Prize for European Poetry Translation in 2003. He has also translated Goethe's novel *Elective Affinities* (OUP, World's Classics, 1994), Kleist's *Selected Writings* (Dent, 1997) and Goethe's *Faust* (Penguin Classics, 2004 & 2009). The Bloodaxe Contemporary French Poets series includes his translations of (with Helen Constantine) *Spaced, Displaced* by Henri Michaux (1992) and (with Mark Treharne) *Under Clouded Skies / Beauregard* by Philippe Jaccottet (1994).

His fiction titles include a novel, *Davies* (Bloodaxe Books, 1985), and three books of stories, *Back at the Spike* (Ryburn, 1994), and *Under the Dam* (2005) and *The Shieling* (2009) from Comma Press. His other books include *Early Greek Travellers and the Hellenic Ideal* (Cambridge University Press, 1984), winner of the Runciman Prize in 1985; a biography of Sir William Hamilton, *Fields of Fire* (Weidenfeld & Nicolson, 2001); and *A Living Language: Bloodaxe/Newcastle Poetry Lectures* (Bloodaxe Books/Newcastle University, 2004).

DAVID CONSTANTINE

NINE FATHOM
DEEP

BLOODAXE BOOKS

Copyright © David Constantine 2009

ISBN: 978 1 85224 821 5

First published 2009 by
Bloodaxe Books Ltd,
Highgreen,
Tarset,
Northumberland NE48 1RP.

www.bloodaxebooks.com
For further information about Bloodaxe titles
please visit our website or write to
the above address for a catalogue.

Bloodaxe Books Ltd acknowledges
the financial assistance of
Arts Council England, North East.

Cover design: Neil Astley & Pamela Robertson-Pearce.

Printed in Great Britain by
Bell & Bain Limited, Glasgow, Scotland.

ACKNOWLEDGEMENTS

Acknowledgements are due to the editors of the following publications in which some of these poems first appeared: *Chimera*, *Dreamcatcher*, *London Magazine*, *Matter*, *Modern Poetry in Translation*, *Oxford Magazine*, *Oxford Poetry*, *Poetry London*, *The North*, *The Reader*, *The Rialto* and *The Times Literary Supplement*.

'Children's Crusade 1939' appears by kind permission of Suhrkamp Verlag and Stefan and Barbara Brecht.

CONTENTS

Photomontage

Against a photograph of the two of them in their eighties
Into the bottom righthand corner of the frame
When he was dead and she was beginning her absence
She set a photograph of herself at eighteen
Black and white, she cut it out
From somewhere, she cut round
Herself so she was nowhere and alone
Laughing. Nobody commented
But there it is and see,
It says, how I looked when you fell in love with me
And I with you and didn't we bear it out
To the edge and over the edge of doom?
Her montage in the dying living room.

Frieze

From blue a white Arcadia looks down
Over the bourg, the river and the silver mud
To a strip of foreground where the dead March grass
Is coming to life again in yellow coltsfoot

And we are wheeling my mother along the estuary,
She is in our midst, we wrap her the best we can
Against the bright snow wind, and flocks of voices
Have entered the space vacated by the sea

And following the tide, four generations of us,
Along the nearest edge of the warming earth
We reach a gate and passing through that gate,
She and her retinue, we are in among

A thicket of horses and she who is losing
All of the names we give to things and creatures
Loses the fear also, there seems no reason
Left anywhere in her to fear a strangeness

And the creatures flair this and are curious
To know a human frail as the moon in daylight
Seated small who lifts a hand (the light
Shines almost through) and not to fend them off

But bless and stroke and pat and have their nuzzling
And kisses. Queen she looks, ancient,
Or fearless girl among the hippocamps,
The crowding shoal of them with musing

Underwater eyes, who bow and lift their long
Heads over her and trail their salt and sticky
Manes and fringes, like the wrack and breakers
Far out on the returning sea, to feel.

If you could hear off the surface of these pictures
The crying of souls over the silver mudflats
You may pick up the conversation now
Engaged between my mother and the beasts,

Their snuffling and flubbering and snorting
And hers a soothing wondering little singsong,
An opened spring of present happiness
From elsewhere, way back, local, home. In me

That tone, the very note of her, revives
A child who offers up the gold of coltsfoot
To a whitehaired woman who inclines
Smiling to thank him from the background blue.

Prayer to the Ghosts

Be definite, come with proofs, speak clearly, ghosts
Be patient with her, in a gentle way
Insist. Though I know all your bodyweight is
Less than a snowflake

And even what small warmth still lives on her face
Would melt you, perhaps at the pulses, perhaps
At the temples or wrists or when she's asleep
Landing on the lids

You who are legion, you I begin to think
Homeless without her, touching, melting, lasting
A while in an after-chill, surely you might
Muster enough and

Cross through the thin skin and enter the thin blood
Of memory, thicken it, be a reminder
Of how to remember, assemble around
Her a lifetime, ghosts.

Moonlights

Both needing cradling, who exactly
They were to one another then
Perhaps we'll never know but only this

For sure (the figures babe-in-arms
And crone
Being brighter than their names): he was

The new moon crescent round and bearing up
The old, she was
The old still clinging visibly to

Her shadow self. As though
A sea of ninety years was nothing vast, as though
Four generations of upheaving waves

Were child's play, little skiff
He made bravely towards
The almost occluded beacon of her face, towards

Her glimmering, her sudden lightning, and they formed
Round either hemisphere
Embracing smiles. The moon

Has many ways of showing. Blessed
Who saw and blessed whoever even heard
On good authority of this:

Her darkness, her incognita, her faded
And coming into plenitude
Body of seas and mountains hooped on facing sides

With light, the waxing light,
The waning, both one moment
Opposite and equal bright.

Franz Xaver Messerschmidt's *Todeskampf*

Now the faces he has left – which were his own
Essaying in a mirror physiognomies
So terrible even merriment looks more
Than humans should ever have to bear – his fifty

Characters clamour for this, his last, the one
He could not do, it was beyond him, even him,
The master howling at us in the studio
Among his fifty heads for the love of truth

You should have cast me as the man trying to die
And not being let. Indeed, we should have, him
Cheyne-Stoking, in his long refusings to be forced
To breathe, in his repeated furtherings of

His bid to die, him holding there, on the lip
Of victory, the hero of apnoea, why
Did we not fix him quick, the skull and visage
Shrunk to a clenching fist and looking breakable

As sparrowframe, the visioning globules swum
Deep into hiding under the eaves of bone, the sullied
Whites left staring, peaky nose and every
Wrinkle round the strict mouth gathered in the act

Of dying? It might have rid us of the ghost
Of him still being fetched by heart and brain, the brute
Mechanics, again, again, again, by yet
Another breath back on the alive with shudderings.

The Mountains in the Mirror

Along that road and I could show you where
Leaving suddenly the mountains appear,
The head and shoulders and skirts of them are there
White on the cold blue in the mirror and it is clear

Without mercy what you are leaving and you know
Those sharply in focus, framed, are only the few
At the hub of a wheel of many more so that the sum
Of loss you turn on is times and times of them.

Paths climbing, streams falling without number
The next bend wipes the place and at your back
You feel the passenger you must chauffeur
Into the flatlands, she is cold, she is wearing black.

Back There

Back in the land
Of rock and tormentil
The lake again
The wreckage made by the ice
And water, water
Lapping, hurrying, hiding
And leaping white
Back under the ravens
In the old domain
I had walked miles
In her close company
With never a word
And my head full
Of our conversations
And when I turned
To speak of something
I should never have seen but for her
There was no one there.

In the cup of my hands
Through sedge and tormentil
I raised the clear water
Of all I had wanted to say
Brimming to her
Absence whose eyes
May be green or blue
But only as the sea
Is both in hastening weather.

I went on alone
Through the works of the ice
Full in the sun
And after some miles
Browsing on hurts
And thinking of her
And what I would say
Or might have said
Cold came over my back
And I knew I might know

Exactly at last
If I turned again
There she would be
As white as Paros
But dewy with the life
And offering me
Under the ravens
Her purple mouth.

Now This

I told you how by an accident
(The reading light left on)
That early nearly winter morning years ago
There was a long black window yellow with them
Soft and throbbing, almost a warmth
For the soul inside
Who was a poor wisht thing all skin and bone.

Now this: the wallpaper
Comes off with triangles of plaster
Like dirty ice, and there's the hemisphere and *arbor vitae*
Dry, the delicate relique
Whorled and marbled, leafing intricately
Chamber to chamber stitched like mail
A drift of seed packed up under the eaves
Flat on, the empty den
Of all the fled imaginings
There all the time
And I never listened.

Had I
Tell me, anima
Anima vagula
And had appeared that early morning not only furred
Against the frost in them
But brain-full also of the whisperings of them
And you in there behind the glass
Despairingly cold and small
Would you have dared
To open to me and insert your hands
Under my outer skin to feel the real
And warm your breasts and belly against me
And clear my eyes to see into
Unclog my mouth and suck from me
All the persuasive wordings I had listened to
Night after night, my ear hard up against
The hearth and very voice of them

Tell me
My animula
Would you have
And would again?

The Ice Statues

Bare hands is the answer, it came to me
Last night, waking at the bad time, staring after
Sleep, the unbiddable:
Warm hands
Eyes that could see the shape in hiding in the lucid block
Faith hot as fire
A melting breath
Little licks and kisses of life.

Born warm-handed
They learned about ice, how thin
The inhabitable warmth is over the curves of the earth
For so much ice and a cold sufficient for ice.
They positioned themselves
Under the greatest possible number of stars
A Siberia full
And employed the spine like a divining rod
To feel for the streams, the rivers, the falls, the lakes, the seas
Of ice.
They learned to discern its lovely impurities
Flaws and fragilities
How it might cleave
Its risks of crack and fracture
And taking delivery
Of a portion about the size of a generous coffin
Or a monkish bed
Began that night
The laying on of hands
In patience until the dew of generation flowed
And they could work at persuading a hill or a hollow into existence
Thumbing in sockets
Easing up a slope with the ball of the thumb
Raking in ribs
Splaying fingers
Fingering in lips
Lending the cup of a palm its fill
And so on
Night after night
At the long design

Warm-handedly from shocked
Head to shivery toe

To stand a company of souls
In cold moonlight
And a barely warmer sunlight
In the public square
The souls unclothed
Skin glistening
And all by virtue of their inner rainbows
Milkiness
Dapples of sky
And ceaseless rememberings of every kind of water
Different
So that the people going about their business
Bulky in furs, with only a slit of vision
Would go in awe and familiarly among them
And learn the look of truthful nakedness
And be encouraged
Month after month of winter.

The Jewels

(Baudelaire)

She I love much was nude except that she,
Knowing my likings, had kept her jewellery on,
Which sonorous gear gave her the mastery
Slaves have on good days over their sultan.

When it flings out its quick and mocking noise
This dancing world brilliant with metal and stone
Ecstasies me, I love to madness those
Things in which light and sound combine and join.

So she lay out on high allowing me
To love her couched up there smiling at ease
Down at my love as deep and gentle as the sea
That towards her, up the cliff-face of her, rose.

Eyes fixed on me, beast in captivity,
In a dreaming absent-mindedness she tried out poses
Whose candour mixing with lubricity
Gave a new edge to her metamorphoses;

And her arms, her legs, her bum, her thighs,
Smooth as oil, swanlike, serpentine,
Displayed to my serene clear-seeing eyes,
And her belly and breasts, grape-clusters of my vine,

Came on more sweetly than the Bad Angel
And troubled the repose my soul had made
And moved her from her crystal pedestal
Where she had sat, calmly in solitude.

In a new design, her buttocks salient,
I seemed to see Antiope's thighs below
The bust of a smooth boy, magnificent
Her fauve and painted duskiness on show

And the lamp having resigned itself to die
Firelight was all the lighting that room had
And sudden flames, exhaling with a sigh,
Coloured her amber skin blood-red.

The Nudist Beach that faces Leper Island

Rise early and you may be shown
The phantoms solid, set in stone
Or ice, the bergs of nightmare, white,
Off-white, the dirty corbie white,
The huddled clan of shapes of heads
Cast on daylight in their hoods

By the levelling sun that soon
Swings away to illuminate
The beach for humans who rise late,
Breakfast on balconies and attend
To nothing but their afternoon
Over there. Leper Island

Fades behind the eyes of the sun
While those who do not wish to be
White arrive and oil and lie
Face in the sand, face to the sky
Presenting, lifting, lolling open
Close to the lisping mouths of the sea

Each visibly being entertained
By thoughts of mixing with its kind
Or whatever might crawl from the throats of the sea.
Like sleepwalkers some stand, display
As though they dreamed in privacy
Viewed through eyelashes and may

Slip off the heat of the sun, slip in
To moiré silks of sea, the skin
Thoroughly cooling, cruise, appraise
All being shown under the gaze
Of Leper Island that has gone
To haunt the back of the head of the sun.

The Virgin, the Monk and the Girls

Down here the Icon of the Virgin landed.
She drifted from Palestine in the days of the breaking of images
And beached here. The girls
When the fancy takes them climb to have a look at her
In the holy eyrie stuck to the cliff
Like mud with the spit of faith. All sunny day
The girls ascend like water through the rock to the Virgin's Well.
They are inspected through a Judas hole
And through an iron grille instructed to cover themselves
And let in under the lintel stooping and hunching
To the one monk alive
Who tells them the story of Mary of the Sea,
The miracle, and shows her to them, she is hung
With as many silver ex-votos
As there are hopes that she will be efficacious
Against the dying of the beauties of the flesh
As he explains. He wears thick spectacles, he peers
Like a bathysphere. He refreshes the girls
With a glass of ice-cold water from the Virgin's Well
And they go down again
Out of the heights he lives in with the Virgin
Into the blue they go
Down as many hundred steps as there are fears of dying
All day there is a ladder of girls ascending,
A cool vein of water, a refreshing chain, all day
Descending again beyond the Keeper of Mary's eyesight
Into the blue, into the sea that carried her
Indifferent from the Holy Land to here
Face up sometimes under the sun and stars
Face down sometimes over the shadows of dolphins
Flotsam on the sea that is older than any Mary
Older even than sea-born Aphrodite
The sea the girls unclothing enter again.

Lethe
(Baudelaire)

Your soul is deaf to mine and cruel but lie
Tigerish, indolent monster I adore,
Here on my heart, I wish to steep and steady
My hands in the heavy thicket of your hair

Or in your skirts, that smell of you, entomb
My head full of the dolorous hurts you gave
And breathe in what's still left of love, its grave
And after-smell, its over-opened bloom.

I want to sleep, more than I want to live,
In a sleep as soft on me as death would be
And lay my kisses like one glad to give
The length of you who are smooth and coppery.

To swallow up my sobbing when it stops
There's nowhere better than your bed's deep pit;
At the waters of your mouth I can forget;
You slip me Lethe through your parting lips.

I will obey my fate, henceforth my bliss,
The way the elect, the predestined, do,
As docile martyr, condemned innocent, who
Self-stokes the hot pyre hotter with holiness;

And drown my bitterness by sucking good
Hemlock and nepenthes at the tart
Points of your tight breasts that never did
Under their charms contain a captive heart.

L'Origine du monde

(after Courbet)

Oh, I forgot,
She said, the rest's
Incognita
And pulled the sheet
Of map up over her
Becoming then
Above the waist
Mare Nostrum
Crossing her heart
Under the caves
Of Thetis and through
The river of Leda
Smiling invisibly

And leaving him
Between the slopes
From hip to knee
And knee to her
Magenta-painted toes
Still deepening
His study of
The intricately
Lipped and lobed
And hooded nest
And den of origins

And seeing all
He saw there shown
As though he showed
Or murmured it
To her: a streaming
Scalded head
Of land raised up
By fire through the sea
Acropolis
And terraces
That overflowed
In scalloped pools
Of lupin blue

And we were there
The pair of us
The strollers through
The asphodels
For centuries
He said she said
And if again
By fire and ice
The sea is raised
The land sunk down
We'll grow our gills
Again, she said
And join the fish
The nosy fish
The warm and smiling
Suckling fish
Who know our kind
Of old, who've seen
Us tesseraed
On rippling floors
And red on black
On fired bowls
In the sealed holds
Of foundered ships.

My dabbler
My just begun
Enquire me more
Deepen me
There's more and more
Under the sea
The Middle Sea
Whose centrique part
Sends circles out
That break upon
The shores around
And tremor through
The sands and snows
There's more and more
I promise you
Crossing my heart
Under the sea
And smiling through.

Finder

My best find – it is behind glass now and hard
To make sense of, I suppose, or have
Much feeling for – was the form, hard as a fossil,

A lamp-shell, say, in the white Cretaceous,
Of a woman's breast, the left, with some
Clavicle and beginnings of the upper arm, just that

Of her, only that, hard as a trilobite's
Carapace kept till now in the grey Silurian mud. I kept it –
Her – on my writing table through the years

Of trying to say what it was like, the thin
Clothing, the *un*clothing, the sleep with my right hand,
My writing hand, casing in flesh and blood

Her breast and the heartbeat quietening and our
Branching apart, finer and finer, our evanescence
Into our timeless dreams. So many nights,

So many early mornings, that relic under the lamplight,
My hand alert and waiting to be prompted
Over the paper, to unharden her,

To whisper like the sea – that had been audible
Whenever there was quiet in her rooms –
And murmur through her hair into the shell the lines

Of lovetalk as they came back to me
Until the heart under my dreaming hand should start again
And the woman turned aside as though to sleep

In the choked house in the last breathing space
Be woken among the airy frescoes
And their illusions of gardens stepping down

On terraces towards the lapping sea
Barefoot, my risen dancer, and her right hand
Would reach to her left shoulder for the fastening.

Helena

(Heine)

You fetched me up by force of the will
Of magic out of the grave.
You heated me with your lust and can't
Quench it now I'm alive.

Fasten your mouth on mine, human
Breath is heavenly stuff.
I'll drink your soul up, every drop.
The dead can't get enough.

The Woman in the House

Anadyomene in the back kitchen
Handed a towel becomes
Woman looking over her shoulder at herself

In the long mirror salvaged from a wardrobe
He chopped for kindling. She becomes
On the rug against the blaze of the black range

Leaning forward the length of her and firelight on her spine
Woman after her bath
Drying her left foot. To be there in this

You would need to go back to the days of a young husband
Incredulous over the woman in the house
Over her things and her activities in every room

And marvelling at his hands. His hands
From seeing via the thudding heart
To the white sheet carried the sight of her

The shock and the quick of the sight of her
Almost without loss. And even now
Sorrowing over his hands

That have become a clutch of twigs and the charcoal
Only another dead twig thrust in among them
He sees like flames

That live for a moment above the body of the fire
On the air, on nothing
Or more like shades, white shades, still fluttering in a thicket

Woman in the bathtub sponging her throat
Woman rising against the ever lithe and joyous flames
Woman bowed and towelling the bared nape of her neck

And woman pouring
The torrent of her hair in the light of hearth and home
For the long, the almost endless combing.

Girl Walking Barefoot

Girl walking barefoot over the crematorium lawns in black
I see you like the feel of the covering of the earth
Green over black and damp, I see
You like the thought of the look of yourself in black
Sauntering over the lawns between the blocks
Of numbered roses. The hearses
Ply like birds with mouths to feed, the parties
Form in the sun like clouds until their own
Hard seeding docks. But you
Girl amble away over the lawns in black
On two crooked fingers swinging your dressy shoes.

Woman on a Swing

Under that dress which is as soft as a moth
Her legs are stiffly together and all he will see
On each incoming is her soles' refusal, flat,
Until she retracts it for the reflux,

Smiling, bending her knees, and lifts against
A hemisphere of sunset that will take
For ever to become decidedly
The night. Time idles, the ticktock is blissful,

Especially the rising away from him
Higher and further, no wonder it's then
She smiles, she's above the earth and for how long
And how high and how fast and close she'll arrive

Again over his set face, that will be her
Doing and all the cradling of yes and no
Hers. She is rocking her life back to the lip
Of the breaking wave of girlhood. Her children

Watch on the sidelines, sourly, they are bored
By the playground, they see that the play has
Nothing to do with them. Warm dusks in the north
Are rare but they last for ever. She is thinking

On the next oncoming she may kick off
One shoe and point with her toes to what
The man there waiting and watching has not seen:
The sickle and wishing moon above his head.

Women Waiting

So many there are by now in shadow down
The lanes, on side-streets, behind the promenade
In the big houses, at the windows, waiting
All day for a caller or at least to wave

At a passer-by. Some days there are none
All day, not one passer-by to whom they might
Have waved and who, for a kindness, might have
Acted along and waved. And even that,

The achieved event, would be nothing or not
What it is they are waiting for but more
A proof they are waiting for nothing at all
Except the caller, theirs. I think they have dressed

The best they can, as well as the rules permit
In what remains. Behind the glass they appear
Like their own reflections, they look as frail
As the old moon does in the afternoon and faint

As creatures who must pit their own resource,
Whiteness, against a sunless cave. They are
Like girls in their day who were always waiting
To be asked, to be called for, to be taken out,

Hopeful at windows but becoming fearful
They would wait and wait and their one resource,
Pale beauty, would fail to draw a caller from
The sea, the town, the busy streets in time.

Lorenzetti's *Last Supper*

Black outside but for a few bright specks
Of redundant universe, the room itself
Lit by haloes and the Christ feeds
The dead star Judas
His lines. It is storytime, they are sitting uncomfortably
On marble sepulchres. Much cosier
Is the cramped kitchen
Next door
With a roaring fire
And the cat lies in a dozy heaven of warmth
And the dog is licking the leavings off the platters of the
        important people
And a couple of scullions are flirting and nattering.

So there always was and is still
Life
And in a room next door the Leader among his men
Big with ideas. Alas for you
Life, the son God hurled
At the earth like an asteroid
And marked the place of impact with a massacre
Will be leaving shortly in darkness at noon
On his long trajectory
Threading suicide, martyrdom, supernovae of killing.

Cranach's *The Golden Age*

Behind an elaborate killing it is understandable
There should be natural beauty wearing
Sparse adornments, man's good work, a road
Climbing in lovely curves to the snow, the col, the blue, but here

Where all the large foreground is the walled garden
Of the Golden Age why lift up our eyes,
Staring where we are now, beyond the wall
To the perched abodes, forts, Houses of the Lord and higher

To the snow, the blue, the passage out of sight? From there,
Surely as iron and lead, will again come down
To do or watch, as they always have, the clever makers,
Planters, breeders, improvers, and at the asylum wall

Setting ladders will view the naked men
And the but-for-their-necklaces naked women, six
Already coupled up and sharing a bunch of grapes,
Discussing pleasure, frolicking in water, six besides

Dancing in a ring around the apple tree, while other
Shoots of creation, a pair of lions, of deer, of rabbits,
And birds on the ground too amorous to fly,
All the kinds together in amity are doing their courting

Among the carnations, the roses, quince and cherry,
Pear, medlar and hazel. Our spectators,
Perhaps corruptible, perhaps beginning to remember
And wonder whether, among them soon will appear

Along the wall three heads of the three chief gods
And say what under scrutiny is to eat and how
To prepare it and what only for crucifixion, breaking,
Stoning, flaying, beheading, and call up the usual

Big codpiece sort to do and at that water
(Come underground from the snow and springing here)
In which that childish pair are splashing blithely
Afterwards will kneel to wash their hands.

Dawn, Noon and Evening
(after Caspar David Friedrich)

Dawn

The watery light in the saturated air
Is sun dissolving as it rises. Might be an hour
Before you see the fire and even then

Flat, white, cold, a thin coin
In appearance like the water-commanding moon.
Shores and forests and bare mountains

Are biding their time of appearance but he, the drylander
Who cloaks his bones in a soft moist skin
Is rocking already on the shallows of an inland sea.

Water is best, and he is mostly water. But now
He must concentrate the light of his mind and his clever hands
On landing fish. I imagine him not even muttering

Encouragements to himself though the soul in him
Fervently wishes he would halloo
Far and high and wide and again and again.

She would love to know whether anywhere around
There is another being at all like her
Inquisitive, sociable, uplifted, always wanting to see

And whether shoving off at dawn into the fog
In a trunk with a pole and a little sail of breath
He is heading towards some society or away.

Noon

As I painted this scene I saw beyond any doubt
We shall never be at home here whatever we do.
Noon was dull, a mild grey, it will not smite you;
And sylvan hasn't meant savage in our land for years;

All's softened; but as I did my copse of trees
They dwindled my two little humans almost to nothing
And the path I made, such a pleasing curve,
Steadily bore her away, far left. I saw

This continuing without me, the trees taller,
Sky damping the earth with fears even at noon,
Absence, all my doing. Little man far right
Cross the dumb field while you can, wish her good day.

Evening

Dawn was dull and noon and the brief afternoon
Dull and the pale light general. Only now
Does the source descend into their vision
And with this moderate effulgence quits them

For ambling along companionably
All day in a dark wood. The last trees stand tall
Like bars but they'll squeeze through and arm in arm
Tumble in glory into the common fosse.

So much for the sheep. Take it from me, Chloë
Goats have more fun. Earth is not lagged all around
With fog, she will unbutton you slowly or
Rip, if you can't wait, the long dress of pale cloud

On pastures of naked sky and as for woods,
The light beech, the dark holm, how your slopes will love
The many textures of bedding. Couple, sleep
And crawl in the morning to the grassy hem

And there, cross my heart, I will show you a light
Giggling with the breezes, flirting with midges
And freshly out of websilk, dew and frogspit
Shape you up desire again, hard as a bole.

Roman Sarcophagus

On its broad surface, under the pitiless clock,
You could have your bowl of oranges, your red
And sooty anemones in a sparkling vase,
The house-keys and the week's unsorted post,

The eats and drinks for a party now and then,
Candles if you like, your foreign money,
Tickets and passport on the morning of a journey.
It makes a solid sideboard. And no, the idea

Of that in the living room doesn't stop my blood,
Quite the opposite, several dead
I'd willingly give them house-room and be glad
They were still there in the many eyes of the marble.

Because, look closely, if that's the life to come
We'd better be training for it now. See how
It's all movement, it's all a partaking of
What you might have liked to be. That nereid

Eyeing you while you frown and bite your nails,
Landlubber, she says, try water next time,
Come and mix with me, the centaur
Pities your lack of horse, and dumb and stodgy

You know yourself to have been when you follow
The running lines of a vine. Remember
Though I loved the sea I was never much of a sailor
So while you are feasting believe I have become

That winged genius, Eros perhaps, with oars
In a little boat with a sail, and seeing what headway
I make among the rollicking hippocamps
Think well if he can with his oars and a sail

And never much of a sailor why shouldn't we
And to us also be given a following breeze
And the help of wings? Flower while there's time,
Learn how, learn more of the forms of life

38

Before you set, the writ of this hard marble
Is quick as water. Because
That seated human who seems to be presiding
Could be anyone, but the tactful figure near him

Hovering as though he did not wish to interrupt
And might be murmuring 'Only when you're ready'
No shadow of a doubt he is Hermes Psychopompus
Who trusts you know the rules.

18 Via del Corso

Incognito here he will become the one he is.
The room looks into the Via della Fontanella,
A promising name, five windows in from the Corso,
Main artery of the blood of carnival

From one of the entrances and bowls of life
Brimming, the Piazza del Popolo.
He fits the city, he has a certain purpose
And he will have in to live with him

Only the deities who help, he wants them appraising
His table and chair, his shelf of books,
His box of manuscripts, his roomy bed. Oh he
Has come here very hungry, his eyes were starving.

So now to hell with martyrdoms and contortions!
To hell with all the sad deposits of the tide of Christ!
The Corso will deliver him straight to the heart's terrain
Of goat, acanthus, fig against the rising moon,

Bucolics, the columns sprouting among the pines,
Wreckage and seedground. Out of the earth
He will lift himself her beauties, his writing hand
Is desirous of learning the other arts. This man sensing

The possibilities of the Via della Fontanella
Believes the point of the earth and her sun and moon and stars
Is him. Every dawn asks him
What will you do for the good of your life today?

26 Piazza di Spagna

Down his right side on the flowered steps
And at his feet in the piazza
From before the birth to beyond the dying of the lengthening days
There is the din the living make

As though his narrow room were faced on those two sides
Like a deep sarcophagus
Life rioting along them in a densely connected frieze,
Centaur, hippocamp, siren, the moving

Between forms, the partaking one of another,
Eyes bright with a purpose in the foliage. He
Cannot sort them now, he cannot rhyme them or scan them
To what they exactly are, the gift has gone,

He lies already heraldic in the hubbub of Chaos,
The bacilli eating his lungs of inspiration
Have stopped his mouth with blood. He suffers noise
And cannot make a music. Only at nights

The hearth of friendship warming his left side
He listens to the fountain in the emptiness
Under the stars, the endless renewing of water
That is like the speaking softly of a constant writing.

He swaps her white carnelian from hand to hand.
He will go under a roof of violets and daisies
(His friend has promised) holding her letters as though
In there he could bear to read them.

Joseph Pitton de Tournefort, Antiparos, 30 July 1700

He was a week down there and looked ghastly
But he spoke at once, still in the coils of rope,
And colour came up in him: Brothers and sisters
I wear on my retinas proof incontrovertible
Of the vegetation of stones. Others have noted
Their dendroid rings of growth, their collyflower
Bunchings and bloomings, but I am the first
Human to witness by powerful candlelight
And live to tell you how they lubricate themselves
For copulation. I saw an extensive floor
All humpy with their silent tendernesses,
A cold glistening, the sheen and feel of silk
Shot through with rainbows. I pinched my flame
And sat in darkness holding two cold rondures
And in my head there was a sudden shooting
Of all that I knew already from the upper earth
Of the vegetation of stones: from talc to diamond
How rich I discovered myself to be in knowledge
Of the carnal touch of stones and of the flowering
They have it in them to perform: the ferns,
The articulated lilies, the leafing gold,
Their veins that carry saps of silver, quartz
And porphyry. But above all I dwelled
There in the pitch black on their slowness,
Their silent patience. Brothers and sisters
Travelling thus on thoughts of generation
And flowerings far beyond our meagre kind
In so much bulk of the earth from deep cave
To ice peak, thinking now of this
Might it not ease us into the slowing down
When we continue without brain or person
And must participate inconceivably
In the fire, the wind, the seas that are the making
Of the lives of stones? Dear brothers and sisters
I surface wishing to quicken us meanwhile,
Freshen our soft fingers to the feel of stones,
Their surfaces, the lives they allow on them,
Brighten our eyes to the flickerings of mica,

For example, and teach our tongues and snouts
To browse delightedly as long as may be
Here under Helios on the bread of stones
Dabbed with the golden, tufted with the glaucous lichens.

All this and more, sipping a little water.

The Floor of the Ammonites

In the small space between the sliding cliffs and the sea
In the small time between the tides
Families come out from the little town to here

Which is as far out as they dare
To view the blue-grey floor of the ammonites
The sea uncovering their solid ghosts

Curling like suns across an earthly firmament
Lives set hard in the appearance of sailing
And the soft feet of the children paddle unharmed

Over their cooled fires. Though sea and feet
And weather coming and going may erase
Some of these strewn rosettes

More they rub into being seen:
More quoits in the long game
More horns and springs and the flung rings of life

And the coils and the cicatrices. Love, that day
Perhaps because evening closed on the viewing and I saw
How far the way was back to the little town

How hard the children must trudge the unending shingle
Leaving the grey sheet of the ammonites
One pocked stratum under the waters of life

Old tourbillions, the badges, forgive me
I entertained the cold temptation of a place
Beyond our farthest voyager

Where every treasured likeness is erased
And shapes and marks and many beautiful reminding signs
Turn under other suns and moons

And show themselves unseen
In a fullness of space and time empty
Of all this love and grief.

The Empty Lock

The level cicatrice, so Roman-straight
Over the fields, didn't worry me, rather
I felt raised up and able to get on
Across the damp pretty fast but that was how

I fetched up where I did, in there, like that
In the old lock, or I might say in here
For I'm still in it wherever I stand,
In the empty lock. I had seen the thicket

Ahead and thought of the woman again
Maybe or thought of nothing, then I was in
The brick slit on the mud floor, gone from sight
Of the pearly sky, in silence sunk into,

And could not move for, the fascination
Of the horror of the millions of bricks
All interfitted without end across
And up black walls. The mud was humped and jagged

Around my feet with things not quite, or still
Uneasily, dead, they blister up and break
Any hour of the day or night, I can
Inventorise the lot. High above me were

The thicket bushes, thriving in the light
And keeping it from me. The walls afforded
Hold for nothing that flowered though for things
That crawled they did. Of course I knew very well

I need only stride forward and I'd be
On higher fields outside, the slit was a halt
En route, for stepping up, but I stood there,
Lie here, wishing for a changeling ancestor

Who'd slide in merrily on a longboat,
Rise on the guggling water, singing out
The knack of it, and go his ways, master
Of all the steps, welcome at every pub.

Bone-dry Night

This bone-dry night, no answer, the starved owl
Eating his heart out, the vixen's spoor of sex,
All the dog wants, locked in a gnarl of ice
I can no longer believe I am the man

Who woke once feeling the icy draught of her
Down my left side as she let herself in
Rasping my face with the frost on her hair
And that I was so warm in five minutes

I hatched her fluttering from her sheath of ice
My fund of warmth, inexhaustible, melting
Her tongue and the lips and mouth between her legs
So that the pair of us luxuriated

To the fingertips and breathed, breathed, until
The owl heard more than his echo, the spoor
Sufficiently dampened, our looking glass
Window on the world throve like a coal forest.

The Winds

Lovely to lie in bed, listening to the rough winds...
TIBULLUS,
Elegies, I.1

I suppose that she slept first and you lay listening
    Until you slept and woke again and listened
To the rough winds and her soft breathing. Roof, four walls,
    The bed, the inspirations. And the contented
Housing of her quietened heart under your hand
    This was the long sweet aftermath of the winds
That you and she, before you slept, had heard arriving
    Out of a source they never would empty
As you would never your conjoined abundance. The winds
    Were more than a likeness, they were the mover
Itself, the conjuror who mated love with pleasure
    And raised you wave on wave until it felt
The winds were you or you were deck and sails at sea
    Or the flues of a house one step from the surf
Or a high wind when it hits a city and in haste
    Through slits and bridges, among domes and towers
In sunny mirrorings, all surprise and dashing,
    Joyously multiplies. My lucky friend,
For love's hyperbole you needed all the tongues
    The four winds learn from friction with the earth.

Prayer to Aeolus

God of the winds, Aeolus, out of your cave
Send me some breath. You undulate oceans,
Snow, deserts and cypresses, fire bides in smoke,
Music in reeds

For you, all things that have any dance in them
Lift when you visit, whatever radius
You ride where you strike is a centre and sings
Out true to itself.

Borrower and generous lender of shapes
Aeolus, among the invisibles you are
Easy enough to believe in and known like
Grief in your absence.

I am leaden, inert, I cannot go out
Into any phenomena, not one life
Can shape or inhabit. Even the waves, I
Lie awake listening

To you and can only imagine the waves
As mechanics, I weigh them down with my own
Repetitive metre, no slant, no lilt, who
Have had them arrive

Skyhigh in a blizzard of spindrift roaring
With you, on and on, in and in, they flung at
My feet and freighted my beckoning arms with
The spring tides of love.

Aeolus, unfasten the mouth of your cave,
Lend me breath before March without mercy asks
On the wintered hillside of love can the black
Thorn blossom or not.

Berlin 1990

When it was over, they raised their stalls in the ruins
Or laid an old army blanket on the dust
To sell off the badges, trophies, medals and orders
All the insignia and paraphernalia
Forty years of it. I watched the arrival of a capacious tourist bus
With darkened windows, like a three-storey limo
And out of it tumbled in white
The West. I remember one beauty
Who tottered in heels across the rubble to the sale
And posed against the wasteland
In a flag and a fur hat.
What chortles on the side of the cameras!
But the sellers were trying out their smiles
Like something they would have to get used to.

Quatrains for a Primer of our Times

(Supply your own images)

Prayer

Assemble again your martyr, Allah of Love,
All his parts and first the private so
That on his virgins he may get above
Angels for the trash he slew below.

Fox News

My name's Brit Hume. I buy and sell. I see
The unspeakable and this occurs to me:
Buy now. Oh when I can't see you for blood
My friend, I think: Futures are looking good.

Communiqué

O gentleman removing from your eye
Material you can't identify
It is the love of Allah you have seen
At work through us, his brave mujahideen.

Woman

Where was I going? I was going to meet the man
I loved and who loves me, to carry out our plan.
He will have been there early at the meeting place
Ever more anxious his beloved face.

Epitaph

We pile here in the usual ratio
Of us to you. So numerous in death
None has a stone and script to lie beneath.
This cicatrice, this bulldozed trench must do.

Fact

The fact is, friend, we matter more than you.
One husband, lover, son, father of ours
Outweighs at least a hundred such of yours.
It's a fact of life, my friend – and of death too.

The Elect

This morning's Rapture Factor's very high.
Today God's Chosen People may, as planned,
Start humankind's last war in the Holy Land.
Hooray for us! The rest of you will fry.

Image Unavailable

No photos yet of the mothers of Iraq
Thanking us for cluster bombs. Must be they lack
The gift of seeing through our Secretary's eyes
And cannot know a blessing in disguise.

Birth Pangs

The school fell on him and he came out blind,
His teacher's in there brained, but never mind:
You don't need brains to know or eyes to see
These are the birth pangs of democracy.

Child

After. Over and done with. All gone.
She is too small to be left on the road alone.
Another day, another night, will nobody come?
Death will, a kindness, and take her home.

Children's Crusade 1939

(Brecht)

War came into Poland
In 1939
And there was only a wasteland
Where house and home had been.

The armies took brother from sister
And man from wife. In the fire
And rubble the child sought the mother
And couldn't find her anywhere.

Then nothing came out of Poland
No newspaper, no post
But a story, a strange story,
Circulates in the east.

In an eastern town snow was falling
When they told the story about
A children's crusade and Poland
Was where it started out.

There were children trailing the long roads
In troops and passing through
The shot-to-pieces villages
Their hungry numbers grew.

They were trying to escape the battles
And all the nightmare
And one day come to a country
Where there'd be no more war.

They had a boy for a leader
He cheered them when they were low
But he was worried, he asked himself
Which way? And did not know.

A girl of eleven dragged along
A little lad of four
And to make him a good mother
All she wanted was no more war.

And on the march was a Jewish boy
With velvet at his throat
And he was used to white white bread
But he found his own two feet.

And two little brothers, great strategists,
Marched in that campaign.
Stormed an empty shed but lost it
To the overwhelming rain.

And one lad sidled along apart
He was the thin grey one.
A terrible blame was eating him:
He came from a Nazi legation.

A musicmaker was with them, he found
A drum in a smashed-up store
But couldn't play it, the rat-a-tat-tat
Would have told the world where they were.

They captured a dog
To kill and eat, they said
But hadn't the heart to do it
So they fed him instead.

They opened a school, a little girl
Was chalking the hard word FRIEND
('I' before 'E') on a busted tank
And never reached the end.

And they did have a concert of music
By a winter stream that roared
And the drummer boy was allowed to drum
Because he couldn't be heard.

A girl of twelve, a boy of fifteen
They had a love affair.
In a house and home the guns had smashed
She combed his hair.

The love couldn't live. The cold came on
Too cold. And tell me how
The little trees should blossom
Under so much snow.

And there was even a war
With another troop of children but
They left off fighting when they saw
There was no sense in it.

And while they were still battling
For a smashed platelayer's hut
The story goes one side ran out
Of things to eat and that

When the other side heard of this they sent
Them a sack of spuds because
The side that has not cannot fight
As well as the side that has.

Also there was a court case,
It proceeded uneasily.
By the shining light of two candles
They found the judge guilty.

And there was even a helping hand
(Help never hurt anyone).
A girl in service showed them
How to bath a little one

But she only had two hours
To teach them the things she knew
Because her master and mistress
Wanted seeing to.

And also there was a funeral
Of a boy with a velvet coat.
Two Poles and two Germans
Carried the coffin out.

Protestants, Catholics, Nazis
Were there to close the grave
And a little socialist gave a speech
On the future of those still alive.

So there was faith and hope
And not only bread and meat
And let nobody blame them for thieving
Who gave them nothing to eat

And let nobody blame the poor man
Who turned them from his door:
When it's fifty it's not self-sacrifice
You need for them, but flour.

You come across two or maybe three
You help them and gladly
But who can sit them down to eat
When they are so many?

In a shelled and rubbled farmhouse
They found a sack of flour.
An eleven-year-old tied her apron round
And baked hour after hour.

They chopped wood for the oven
Stirred and kneaded the dough
But they couldn't get it to rise because
None of them knew how.

The best they could, they were heading south.
South is where you see
The sun at noon, it is straight ahead
When there's any sun to see.

They found a wounded soldier
In a pine wood. There he lay.
They tended him for seven days
So he'd show them the way.

He said they should head for Bilgoray,
There was fever in his wound.
He died on them on the eighth day
And they dug him into the ground.

And of course there were still signposts
Though muffled under snow
But all turned round so they didn't point
The right way to go.

And that was for military reasons
And not in cruel fun
But how should they find Bilgoray
In the wrong direction?

They stood around their little leader.
Snow filled the air.
He peered ahead and pointed:
It must be over there.

One night they saw a fire.
They kept away. And then
Once three tanks went rolling by
With human beings in.

And once when they came near a town
They made a detour round
And hid by day and walked by night
Till the town was left behind.

Where south-east Poland used to be
The fifty-five children
Were seen in drifts and driving snow
And then never again.

When I close my eyes I see them
Trekking on and on and on
From one farmstead to another
Shelled-to-pieces every one.

And above them in the clouds I see
New larger crowds, they process
Against the cold winds toilingly
Homeless, directionless

Looking for a land of peace
Without thunder, without the fire
Not like the land they are coming from
They are more and more and more

Vast numbers and in the twilight
I see that they have become
The children of every race and clime
Who want peace and a house and home.

In Poland that January
A dog was caught, it had
A cardboard round its scraggy neck
With writing on that said:

Please help us, we are lost.
We can't find the way any more.
We are fifty-five, the dog will lead
You to where we are

And if you can't come, drive him away
Don't shoot at him, he is
The only living creature
Who knows the way to us.

The writing was a child's.
Peasants read it aloud.
That was a year and a half ago.
The dog hungered and died.

Choruses for Saint Lucy's Day

1

King Oedipus, he saw too much
He had an eye too many perhaps
He saw so much he could not bear
The look of his face with his eyes still there

And stabbed them. But there was in him
Another eye, a Cyclops eye,
That under the sun, under the moon
Sank and filled and rose again

Full of sights so he still wept
Through the empty holes, imagine that,
At things the eye inside him saw
Down there in him, the bathysphere

Day by day and night by night
The silver bucket of his sight
Scooped up things he could not bear
To contemplate. The world outside

The polis still was beautiful
And through it blinded Oedipus
Felt his way and could not close
The eye of the unbearable.

2

Monstrous a lot
But nothing so monstrous
As this that a child
Becoming a biped
Stands up with the world at her feet
To begin her adventures
And almost at once
Scarcely begun
Encountering you
And raising to you

Eyes that believe
You friendly you prove
Her wrong. Believe me, friend
It were better for you
You were sunk out of sight
Headfirst with a rock at your throat
And tolled with the tides
A clapper for crabs
Than have done what you did
To her look that believed you kind.

3

The retinas took it
Can't be deleted
And here you come
Light in our darkness
Saint of our winter
Offering us more.
Must we see more?
Better you gave us
Deeper darkness
Sleep without dreams
Oh unseeing sleep
For a while at least
A passage of winter
Sealing the eyes
Quietening the heart
Almost to stopping
Sinking our heat
Almost to zero
But here you come
Like that girl on the tube
With stumps, that boy
Who could barely see over our table
That dot on the pavement
And offer us eyes
On a platter
Gratis.

4

Girl, will it help to learn from us
Here mouthing again
Eternally treading the sidelines again and again
To learn from us
The wringers of hands
The peepers through horrified fingers, that you
Are not the first
And won't be the last?
Will it help? It will not
But listen.

There was a man, a dreamer
A builder of beautiful buildings
To live in, to work in, it lifted the mind
Even to think of
Their windows, the air
Came playing, the hills and the waters
Welcomed them. So
(It follows) Tyrannus said
Build me one good, one better, the best
And he did as he must and when he had done
And Tyrannus saw it was good
You know what they did
Tyrannus's men
When Tyrannus saw that his home was the best?
What he said they must.
They cooled a rod
With a scream and a hiss
In the builder's eyes
So he would never
For anyone else
Build anything like. Does that comfort you, girl?

It was after your time. It goes on and on.
Hear of another
Long after your time.

There was a woman, an actress
Good at her art, the best in her day
Beloved and Tyrannus sat
Night after night front row in his sepulchre suit

With his men and watched. And he saw
How long she had watched, how much she had seen
Suffering the tyrants, exciting them
Their hands on her throat, oh marrying them
How much she had learned. He saw
How once at least in every performance she paused
Like a gap in the surf
Between wave and wave
Of incoming verse
And looked
The thinking look
The what-do-you-think-about-that sort of look
And all of the eyes in the dark at his back
Were looking at hers
Her seeing face, her omniscient eyes
That had played every part
And behind her eyes
Was a woman who knew. You know what Tyrannus
Did? He rose from his seat
When the show was done
And ascended to her on stage in the public view
And gave her roses
Heavy as twins
An armful of roses
Flown in from wherever the last red roses grew
And bowed and left
Immaculate white
In his evening wear and up came his men
And there and then
Everyone watching
His men with knives
Cut out her eyes.

You are not the first.
You won't be the last.
The show goes on.

Three Notes on *Lear*

Edgar

Bedlam begins at the garden gate.
The King did not know this but Edgar did
Who perhaps had grown up lonely
And stood there often to see them coming from the tombs
Cutting themselves, legion. He saw them feelingly.
And I suppose he had a nurse from among the poor
Closer, who told him the truth in bedtime stories
And scraps of lullaby into nightmare. Easily
He became Poor Tom, fished deep
And as in posh old people after a stroke
Up came the vernacular, the dirt, the baby talk,
The horrors. So he acted in truth
And pretty soon added this to the facts at his disposal:
That worse than bedlam may come up the garden path
As guests, as a lord and lady
And befoul the living room beyond any catharsis
And turn out the host with holes that were his eyes
To be contemplated by his son
Edgar, survivor.

The Word

Give the word. Get it right.
Get it wrong, the portrait of your sainted mother will fall in smithereens
The French windows will blow open and in the glacial draught
All faces present will set in one or other of the possibilities:
Terror or murderous rage. Say the wrong word
All simples ever after will be ineffectual.
Too late. Best, if you are not the person challenged
Should there be a pause while whoever is deliberates
Decamp over the garden wall. Bedlam is kinder.
Their meat is rats and mice, their drink crawling, the wind
Stilettoes through their ribs, but better
This accommodation than the big house.
In bedlam they sprig their veins with rosemary.

Hysterica passio

All the mothers are dead and of them only one,
The Bastard's, gets much of a mention:
She was good sport under the dragon's tail.
The surviving wombs are in the care of their father, an unfit person.
He has the king's evil, his touch is mortal.
Soon he finds himself pregnant, he has no idea how.
It swells up in him, he orders it back down.
But labour is not like that (altogether he has no idea),
Begun is begun, the King is beginning to teem,
King Malediction is bringing forth a mother of his own
Hysterica passio
Who never knew he was so deep with sorrow.
The waters break through his mouth, irrevocable.
No one can bear to look at the mother he brings into the world.
It is a tangle of fiends, six of them he names Kill
Four Howl, and the last out
Never, Never, Never, Never, Never.

Pity

Pity we killed all the monsters. It might have been
A help to ask a sphinx or a centaur,
A siren, a deep-sea triton or some such cross between
Our miserable species and another
What it feels like. Too late now. Goodbye
Creation, we are all going to die.

Our tinnitus is in the five oceans, the air
Spasms with our constant jabber, our shit trails
Eternally in icy space but here we are
Still ignorant beyond our broken fingernails.
All's in the sights of the camera and the gun
But we've no neighbourhood, no conversation.

Dying from the centre, if we still had a rind
Of greenmen, ariels, mermaids, beings that passed
Through into knowledge of some other kind
We might not be killing and dying quite so fast.
We seed our hard selves over the countryside.
Don't play with us. All who did have died.

Nine Fathom Deep

(after Gustave Doré after Coleridge)

Couched where they are, on the seabed
They feel no colder for the draught of the ship
And the glacial spirit passing over them. Lucky you
Say the living dead, to have got

Into the harbour of one another's arms
Not having lodged behind your lids
The rotting sea, the dead hands working nor conceived
Remorse, remorse, the canker.

Love, luckier still, we shall imagine this pair
Nine fathom deep are dreaming
One dream, the hooves of nightmare are battering
Round and round in their encircled hearts

But they wake, they open, and the crime dissolves,
No one needs shriving, nobody
Must trudge through the frontiers of a sickened world
Spouting horrors, but by these lovers waking

The good ship sets her sails, the ice opens
And ahead goes the white bird, friendly and clever
And is the selfsame bird we every morning
Called and it came and showed us more

Than we deserved what grace is like
Wheeling on wings very near, very high
Very near again, oh on the strength of this
The man and woman waking and their astonished eyes

Viewing a clean ship whispering down
The arcades of ice, with a kick
Will freshen the sea, unharm the inhabited earth
And surface like flyers in a rush of bubbles

And every man jack of us will imagine children at home
He will go on his knees to and be level with
And into whose wide eyes and open mouths
He will tell tales as true and nourishing as loaves and fishes.

Melangell

Dead end as hard as a horseshoe, higher
Than any steeple, behind her back
The rains of that region, interthreading,
Dangled down and she sat reading
And in a pause between page and page
On the lap's instinct, on her opening skirt,
The hare landed. Hunted into that cwm
Unless it could climb the rapunzel plait
Nothing lived. But the hare lay under her hand
Facing out and above its eyes
Hers outfaced the dogs and the men.
Silence. Water. Silence. Eyes.

She had closed her book in her right hand
And under her left was the creature's head
And in her lap its drumming heart.
But when was terror sufficient dissuasion?
Oh you would question the world's rivermouths
And climb, life long, all the tributaries
To find through alder, willow and hazel
A terminus under the plaited rain,
A cwm, a lap, where the reader sat
With the shuddering hare in her skirt and its eyes
Afforced by hers in silence started
Mercy in dogs and weaponed men.

Mornings in Maytime

Birdsong no sooner quietening come
The shouts again from over the asylum wall
Echoing in the abyss of the upper air. So his day begins
Howling in mine. Early as now, not all that long ago

On such a May morning I slipped free
From among the sleepers and in the dewy sun
Shivering made into Cwm Pennant without fatigue
And pretty soon heard rising a merriment of children

Higher, ahead of me, hootings and whistlings,
Mewings like buzzards, chuckles and rushes
As though the springs of the wide hillsides
Piped exuberantly into our foreign language

Rainforest strange, the tones warped from the normal,
Slanting home, and I climbed with the sun into a holy
School of holidaying children held up there
For the sky to witness in the hollow of a hand

Of humankindness, kids simple, one way or another
Born awry, the slow, big-eyed, who smile amiably
On everything that lives, the jumpy as hares
And those on whom the sky would fall in pieces

But for their spells, that morning in Maytime
In the arms of an empty valley from a high playground
They cried themselves out loud
And I passed through their interlude of freedom

Carrying the echoes with me into a wood
To the gap where the bearers in the old days
Rested the dead going over for burial
In spring after the snow had kept them locked at home.

Fishing over Lyonesse

(for Hugh Shankland)

Out beyond Hangman Island, out beyond Badplace
   Here at the mouth there's a drop the line wound out
And zinging diagonally down won't fathom
   And I always think of the poor soul alone
On the wide wide sea, too long alone, and of our
   Amiable believer in Atlantis
Who rowed out over a possible upheaval
   In 1712 and the boiling water
Uncaulked his boat. No danger of that, the deeper
   Out here, the colder. Carry on talking, Hugh
While I hold us broadside on to North America
   Across a gap. Down the trembling line
The fish may be listening in to what holds humans
   Together, what keeps them from disassembling
Over depths well known to be unfathomable. Friend,
   Keep talking of dead mothers and fathers
And the living children and their children while I keep
   An eye on the weather, entertain me
And the curious deep fish, I see more clearly
   Where we are, in relation, how much we need
Mutual aid, the telling of stories and to wrap
   Our precious dead and our precious living close
In a welcoming house, Atlantis on dry land,
   The good and peaceable, cheerful, funny,
Close and ordinary. My dear friend with a gift
   For drawing people how they look when only
The angel's watching, the fish have eavesdropped long enough
   And up the taut phone line I've taken to heart
Again what it is I have to learn from the depths
   And now it's cold, we're far out, let the fish be,
Back home there's wine and baking bread, let's land before
   There's worry. Keep talking, tell me all you can
What the dead did and what the living are up to
   And I'll pull my hardest down the channel home
Against the soft beginnings of a drifting mist
   And the little breeze that wants the wide wide sea.

On a Small Island

On a small island when the wind comes in unkindly
There's always a lee, ten minutes
And we can be lying together somewhere else
Conversing easily, layer by layer
Shedding what we had to wear on the weatherside
And let the Furies hurtle over us
Hard as they like to the couldn't-care-less horizon.

The Silence between the Winds

The silence between the winds is very tempting.
Small fire over there, the smoke rises unperturbed.
I open a window, a butterfly wishes to risk it.
The forecast is unequivocal:
They are shifting a few degrees from Siberia to the Arctic
The winds. But see
How all things cannot help remembering
What they like doing in still weather. See
They lift up, look around. The wise
Sit tight, of course, their only pleasure
Judging which of the unwise think this will last for ever
And which know it won't, degrees
Of look, of haste,
Of licking the lips for tempest.

Lost at Sea

We suppose, he left
Our cheerful fug
No worse for wear
Than often before
And under the lintel
And over the threshold
That afternoon
Knowing the tides
And the way to wade
Went into a mist
As thick as a bag.

These islands camp
Like wagons for the night
And all within
Shallows and landmarks
Home. He stepped
At one of the gaps
Into the river of sea
Where the banks are close
As often before
Warm in his aura
Of fags and beer
In fog as thick as a shroud.

The sea is everywhere
Under the window
Along the wall
It salts the gardens
It rides on the air
Especially at nights
We taste of it.
Foreign or local
Ignorant or sussed
Put a foot wrong
And out of our midst
The water takes you
As cold as Styx.

A long disappearance
Weeks, months
And no one likes
To chisel a stone.
The sea is shapeless
Or every shape.
Where is its mouth?
Where are its paws?
It moves you along
When you lodge it bides
Does something else
For a while, you are shelved
Then it fetches you
With a nudge and a shove
And on you go.

The land stacks up
On its contour lines
To nothing compared
With its going below
Big step by step
When you think how the heart
Of a swimming man
Stops at the hints
Of the deep that cruise
In here from beyond
That mouth of the river of sea
Where there's always a swirl
Of noise and it's never
One second still.
Gannets impact
Like arrowheads
But it's nothing at all
Their height of fall
And penetration
Compared with below
Where the drinker drifts
Who is less and less
Himself and more
And more like a log
And all his mind
The rememberer

And stash of dreams
Gone in a run
Of bubbles into the fog.

And all's the same
The sun and moon
Exchange their views
The wind, the light
Play on and on
And the clarities
Are vaporised
But come again
And would hurt the eyes
Of anyone waking out there.
And 'Lost at Sea'
Is better than
'At Peace', 'At Rest'
'Asleep', the sea
Never sleeps
Is never at rest
Has no peace
Gives none, and he
Drifting alone
Is like a draught
Coming under the door
Through bar and snug
A cold whiff
Of the river running
A step away
The river of the sea
That hurries through
The crack in our camp
And carries off
All manner of stuff.

Seaweeds

The seaweeds that had flopped and lain
Dejectedly under the sun
Are lifted now and stretching in
And on salt water have again
Through and through and in between
Wellbeings all their own.

That wrack's a good example: how
It spreads its nubbled fronds and plays
Over the surface to and fro
Fingeringly as the breeze
And the in and out of ripples please.
Only mechanics, I suppose.

However, since the maths applied
In that caressing hand exceed
My head by far I am content
To watch a sentient thing allowed
To feel again and for a tide
To revel in its element.

Evening Primroses

They open the way this little porth
Fills up under the window:
Quietly unstoppably, but are

Not pulled by the moon, the dullest twilight
Works them deep enough
And the damp imago clambers into the air.

This I had patience for, this I could watch
Through all the starts and restings
And even when they looked to be hovering on witholding

Then my credence
That I had feared dead in its clamped shell
Beckoned them further out.

It bowed me again into the aura of your face
Again into the scent of what it feels like
When love, frail thing,

Forces itself into being seen, the unstoppable
Helpless, the unbelievable
Beginning to be believed

Whose opening scent is like
Warmth off the moon
Or the cold off your face when you entered my house and home

Sweet love, sweet breath of it
From these tall flowers, from their pale faces
Opened on the air, earthy.

Fishing

The drowned go out there. But the wind
That day, the little breath of it, and tide
Were motioning in. I was lying just this side
The drop, cradled, with an unquiet mind.

Hot afternoon. By all I understood
Of wind and tide the feathers, hooks and lead
Must strain their leash for home. But no. I paid
More out, yard after yard, and seemed to feed

A hunger in the open sea, I listened down
The long tense strumming slant of line
Into a pit of breathlessness and through

One crooked finger I began to feel
Myself descending a diagonal mile
Over the lip, out deeper, beckoning you.

Owls and Foxes

Hear the owls, little sister
Rhyming across a distance
So clear their wishes

We should not be listening

And the foxes yapping and squealing
So shamelessly

We should not be here listening.

Owls and foxes on a night like this
Under a moon as white as the hard snow
The stars spicules of ice
And the music of the spheres a very brittle ringing
What hearts of warmth they must have
Under fur and feathers.

We should not be lying here listening to the cold.
We should be cast out scavenging in the gardens
Fearful of daylight and civility
Trying will the heart survive
Without fur or feathers.

But listen, feel
How warm it makes us
Lying here listening to the lyrical owls and the lewd foxes.

Chatterer

My warm man, unglove your hand
On a winter mountain and reach for his bare hand
It feels like a small rough animal
Of body heat. He is good in bed
For thawing your toes, he takes them
In at the top of between his thighs and nothing
Delights him more than warmly eclipsing
Your cold bum. Strange then
How he chatters afterwards
This warm creature, the teeth in his head
As though he had gulped a gallon of ice
The way a fire-eater
Does fire by force of will, clenching himself
And what you can hear on the pillow next to you,
Both of you warm, hand-in-glove warm, I tell you
That raddling cold, that clatter of shards of ice in the bucket of
        his head
As though he were hugging nothing but himself
Naked on the bare mountain, that clacking sound
Is him unclenching, him not trying any more
After the warming, it makes me smile, I don't mind telling you
I drift away sleeping smiling to myself
Over the secret of that warm man of mine.

Lilith's Children

Spawned in water how should this love be otherwise
Than teeming? Some nights
In the waking whirlpool, the nearest I get to stillness,
Between two rapids of dreams
It feels like Lilith's children
Howling around for a warmer life in me.
She was so fecund, so lubricious
The wishes of life in her exceeded the cast of sperm.
There is always more to say
There are not enough dots and strokes to make up the letters
To make up the words
To say. Both of us plural
And multiplying
We spawned in water
We milted the rivers and the seas
You and I
We shall haunt the globe
As summer mist off the sea, our seed
Will keep in the ice.

Horse Chestnuts

I knew one let go
Suddenly a vast limb, thinking
Sooner that, a third of me,
Than all and leafed the best he could
Over the splinters. Another I visit
Half a mile away on much the same terrain
Feeling unbearable weight decided otherwise and allowed
Three or four big arms very slowly
To the earth and there they settled
Rooting and in time put up
Tall offspring and she
Continues at the centre, undepleted.

Hawthorns

The house emptied
A human lifetime ago but they
Who can't deracinate themselves
Have stuck it out up here. Kindling
Trickled to the dead hearths from the jackdaw nests, the roof
Vomited in, the gable end
Leaned musingly over its footings till it fell but the hawthorns
Held on, set with the wind and wear
Their own scant blossom, their own few berries
Together with sheep's wool, snow and frozen rain
As though the vanished gypsies
Still visited and hung the lucky trees. The stars up here
Any winter night are harder, brighter, far more definite
Than that faint haze of town
On the flatlands where the spring ends in the dirty rivermouth.

Plum Trees

Like us they want to continue. This example
Foreknowing particular extinction, heaved
All it had left of a self
Wide-open into a quivering and colossal final call
For pollination. The best I can do now
For these exhausted veins in a brittle skeleton
That lifts from among the living without resistance
In the April after is recall
The throb of bees, the mounded
Trug on the girl's bare arm, the bloom, her skin, the groove
Opening on honeyed flesh, the sealed
Inside lozenge, recall
My tree's last fling, outdoing a lifetime, glorious
Bid for a white new forest of its kind.

Mandrake

Mandrake springs from the seed of a hanged man,
Fruits on the ground in hard little apples
And these you may steal easily if you are quick-fingered.
But if it's the root you want, beware.
Approach in a trench, loosen around with your tines,
Noose the creature and fasten the rope to the collar of your dog,
Man's best friend, he trusts you. Walk away
And at thirty paces whistle him.
Out comes your mandrake, the forked thing, with a scream!
Bury your dog whom the act infallibly kills
And feed the rooty fellow to your helpmeet, Eve
And on the mandragora that she will brew for you
Sleep as thick as you can,
Lessen the scream, lessen the weight of the corpse of your black
   hound,
Strengthen, if you can, against the time
When the need to do it again will spring in her and you.

Elm Seeds

That summer when there were still enormous elms
The seed of them drifted over the asphalt, dots
Of another life in a wispy carrier
To a wall or kerb. I saw
Your bare toes in a pleasant density of seed.

So strange the casting of seed over the concrete:
Down it comes twirling
On to a surface that cannot foster it
Or parachutes in as delicate as a snowflake
With no better chance. But of all this bounty
Of fruitless offering and arrival
I will always love best the seed of the vanished elms
Some carried to bed in your sandals and in your hair.

NOTES

Franz Xaver Messerschmidt's *Todeskampf* (14)

Franz Xaver Messerschmidt (1736-83), a German sculptor best known for his 'character heads'. Among the fifty or so that have survived there is no *Todeskampf* (death agony), though that would have been a suitable subject for his violently expressive art.

Cheyne-Stoking: after John Cheyne (1777-1836), Scottish physician, and William Stokes (1804-78), Irish physician. 'The typical Cheyne-Stokes respiration is that in which, after a complete pause, there is gradual return of breathing and increase of chest movements till they attain an exaggerated degree... and again a gradual subsidence and pause' (*OED*). People dying sometimes breathe like that.

Back There (16)

Hurts, another name for whortleberries.

The Jewels (22) and Lethe (25)

'The Jewels' (Les Bijoux) and 'Lethe' (Le Léthé) are two of the six poems removed by the censor from Baudelaire's *Les Fleurs du mal*.

Finder (28)

In 'Finder' I was thinking chiefly of Sir William Hamilton (1730-1803), British Ambassador in Naples, and his interest in the buried cities of Pompeii and Herculaneum.

Helena (29)

Heine's 'Helena' appeared in his *Neue Gedichte* of 1844.

The Woman in the House (30)

Anadyomene, the word means 'rising up' and is used as an epithet of Aphrodite as she rises from the sea or from her bath.

Lorenzetti's *Last Supper* (34)

Pietro Lorenzetti's fresco *The Last Supper* (1320-30) is in the San Francesco Basilica in Assisi.

Cranach's *The Golden Age* (35)

The Golden Age, painted *c.* 1530 by Lucas Cranach the Elder.

Dawn, Noon and Evening (36)
Caspar David Friedrich painted his *Times of Day* (actually four) around 1822.

Roman Sarcophagus (38)
Psychopompus: Hermes in his capacity as conductor of souls to Hades.

18 Via del Corso (40) & **26 Piazza di Spagna** (41)
Goethe arrived in Rome at the end of October 1786, determined to live as he wished. He registered with the authorities under an assumed name, as a German painter: Filippo Miller, *tedesco, pittore*. Keats arrived in Rome in November 1820. He died there the following February. The carnelian was a leaving present from Fanny Brawne. The two houses, 18 Via del Corso and 26 Piazza di Spagna, are ten minutes' walk apart.

Joseph Pitton de Tournefort, Antiparos, 30 July 1770 (42)
Joseph Pitton de Tournefort (1656-1708) was a French traveller, botanist, physician and a believer in 'the vegetation of stones'.

Quatrains for a Primer of Our Times (50)
My model was Brecht. His *War Primer* (*Kriegsfibel*) consists of about 70 photographs with accompanying quatrains. He referred to them as 'photo-epigrams', the image (often with its own text) and his quatrain making up an artistic unit. Brecht put the book together in exile during the Second World War, many of the photographs coming from *Life* magazine.

Children's Crusade 1939 (52)
Brecht's 'Children's Crusade 1939' (Kinderkreuzzug 1939), was first published in 1942. But he returned to it many times and it exists in different versions.

Melangell (66)
Melangell, an Irish princess, became a hermit and a saint in Wales. The huntsman was Brychwel Ysgithrog, a prince of Powys. After this confrontation in 604 he gave her the valley to be a place of sanctuary.